THE STORY OF THE
MEMPHIS GRIZZLIES

THE NBA:
A HISTORY
OF HOOPS

THE STORY OF THE
MEMPHIS
GRIZZLIES

NATE FRISCH

CREATIVE EDUCATION

Published by Creative Education
P.O. Box 227, Mankato, Minnesota 56002
Creative Education is an imprint of The Creative Company
www.thecreativecompany.us

Design and production by Blue Design
Art direction by Rita Marshall
Printed in the United States of America

Photographs by Corbis (NIKKI BOERTMAN/Reuters, Steve
Lipofsky, Albert Pena/ZUMA Press, TIM SHARP/Reuters),
Getty Images (Bill Baptist/NBAE, Andrew D. Bernstein/
NBAE, Walter Bibikow, Gary Dineen/NBAE, Andy Hayt/
NBAE, Fernando Medina/NBAE, Layne Murdoch/NBAE,
Joe Murphy/NBAE, Thinkstock, Jeff Vinnick/NBAE, Rocky
Widner/NBAE), Newscom (Mark Halmas/Icon SMI)

Library of Congress Cataloging-in-Publication Data
Frisch, Nate.
The story of the Memphis Grizzlies / Nate Frisch.
p. cm. — (The NBA: a history of hoops)
Includes index.
Summary: An informative narration of the Memphis
Grizzlies professional basketball team's history from its
1995 founding in Vancouver, British Columbia, to today,
spotlighting memorable players and events.
ISBN 978-1-60818-435-4
1. Memphis Grizzlies (Basketball team)—History—Juvenile
literature. I. Title.

GV885.52.M46F75 2014
796.323'640976819—dc23   2013038291

CCSS: RI.5.1, 2, 3, 8; RH.6-8.4, 5, 7

First Edition
9 8 7 6 5 4 3 2 1

Cover: Guard Mike Conley
Page 2: Guard Jerryd Bayless
Pages 4&5: Guard Mike Conley
Page 6: Forward Mike Miller

TABLE OF CONTENTS

COURTSIDE STORIES

INTRODUCING...

CANADIAN BEGINNINGS

FROM PRIVATE CRAFT TO BARGES, THE MISSISSIPPI RIVER TEEMS WITH TRAFFIC IN MEMPHIS.

Perched upon a wooded bluff overlooking the mighty Mississippi River, Memphis, Tennessee, was both beautiful and productive when it was founded in the early 1800s. The humid, subtropical climate was ideal for growing cotton, and the river provided a means of transportation and distribution. A century later, the city reinvented itself as a musical mecca where artists such as Elvis Presley and Johnny Cash launched their careers.

For decades, the musical culture of Memphis provided entertainment for locals and tourists alike, and the University of Memphis Tigers athletic programs were a source of pride in the city. But it was not until 2001 that a major professional sports franchise would call Memphis home. The new arrivals were the Memphis Grizzlies of the National Basketball Association (NBA).

The name "Grizzlies" was not especially appropriate for a

VETERAN SWINGMAN OTIS THORPE BROUGHT EXPERIENCE TO THE YOUNG GRIZZLIES SQUAD.

Tennessee-based club, but these bears had been born in Vancouver, British Columbia. Lumbering into the NBA in 1995, the new franchise was owned by local businessman Arthur Griffiths. He hired Stu Jackson as the Grizzlies' first president and general manager, and then brought in former Atlanta Hawks assistant coach Brian Winters as the team's first head coach.

With the bigwigs in place, Vancouver set about filling in the roster. It selected 13 players from existing NBA teams via an expansion draft, having to split the spoils with fellow Canadian expansion team, the Toronto Raptors. The most notable additions were fiery point guard Greg Anthony and athletic swingman Theodore "Blue" Edwards. Vancouver came away with some perimeter talent, but it lacked interior

bruisers befitting the title "Grizzlies." The team addressed that issue in the 1995 NBA Draft, selecting Bryant "Big Country" Reeves—a 7-foot and 275-pound country boy from Oklahoma State University.

Reeves had a strong inside game and a willingness to learn that earned praise from coaches and scouts around the league. "I've always liked his game," said Bill Walton, a former All-Star center and television analyst. "He's learned the physical part of the game. All the raw material, all the potential, is there."

Although Reeves and his teammates shocked the NBA by winning their first two games of the 1995–96 season, reality soon set in. The Grizzlies lost their next 19 and would later suffer an NBA-record 23 straight losses en route to a 15–67

THE BIRTH OF A BEAR

When businessman Arthur Griffiths started the process of bringing a professional basketball team to Vancouver, British Columbia, in 1995, he intended to call the new club the "Mounties," after the Royal Canadian Mounted Police, who wear striking red uniforms, wide-brimmed hats, and tall, leather boots. But the real Mounties objected to the use of their name for the team. So Griffiths and Stu Jackson, the team's president and general manager, had to go back to the drawing board, where they came up with the name "Grizzlies." The name seemed apt because grizzly bears roam parts of the rugged landscape of British Columbia. The big animals also reflected a powerful nature, which is always desired in sports, as well as the heritage of western Canada. When the Grizzlies moved from Vancouver to Memphis, Tennessee, in 2001, many people thought the name would have to go. Polls taken in Memphis, however, indicated that fans did not want the name changed. Only the color of the logo and the uniform was modified, from Naismith (neon) blue to Memphis Beale Street blue.

BRYANT REEVES

Bryant "Big Country" Reeves was a dominating presence, a seven-foot giant who could impose his physical will on the court. Reeves came from the tiny town of Gans, Oklahoma, where there are no hotels and where, Reeves said proudly, "We still don't even have a stoplight." This country boy with the buzz cut was selected by the Grizzlies in 1995 as their first-ever NBA draft pick. He had a solid rookie season and then stepped up his game in 1996–97, averaging 16.2 points a night, which earned him a 6-year, $61.8-million contract. But this contract came back to haunt the Grizzlies as Reeves struggled with weight and injury problems. Prior to the 1998–99 season, he reported to training camp 40 pounds over his ideal playing weight, and in 2001, a nagging back injury forced Big Country to retire. "I am grateful to the entire Grizzlies organization for their support ... throughout my career," Reeves said. "Playing in the NBA allowed this small-town country boy ... to share the court with the greatest players in the game."

"THE LOSING HAS BEEN TOUGH. THE ONLY THING
I CAN CONTROL IS MY EFFORT AND MY ATTITUDE
GOING FORWARD.... YOU DO YOUR BEST, KEEP ON
FIGHTING, AND KEEP ON BATTLING."

— SHAREEF ABDUR-RAHIM ON 1996–97 SEASON

finish. Still, Vancouver fans appreciated the nightly effort of their undermanned Grizzlies, packing General Motors Place for nearly all the team's home games.

Jackson set out to reward those fans' faithfulness by obtaining some help for Reeves. Before the 1996 NBA Draft, the Grizzlies traded for forward Pete Chilcutt. Then, with the third overall pick in the Draft, Vancouver selected versatile, 19-year-old forward Shareef Abdur-Rahim from the University of California. After the Draft, the team traded again to obtain forward George Lynch and sharpshooting guard Anthony Peeler.

bdur-Rahim was an immediate sensation. Combining nimble spin moves with a soft shooting touch, he paced the 1996–97 Grizzlies in scoring with 18.7 points per game to earn a place on the NBA's All-Rookie team. Still, Vancouver continued to lose in bunches, again limping to the worst record (14-68) in the NBA. "The losing has been tough," Abdur-Rahim said later. "The only thing I can control is my effort and my attitude going forward.... You do your best, keep on fighting, and keep on battling."

After two such dismal seasons, the Grizzlies hired a new head coach, Brian Hill. The Grizzlies then selected point guard Antonio Daniels with the fourth overall pick in the 1997 NBA Draft. Daniels was slower than the typical point guard, but he also played with unusual determination, and the Grizzlies were willing to take a chance on him. However, he turned out to be a bust, and in 1998, the Grizzlies selected point guard Mike Bibby from the University of Arizona with the second overall pick of the NBA Draft. Bibby, a great ball handler who cared more about giving his teammates scoring opportunities than padding his own statistics, quickly established himself as an elite player, averaging 13.2 points and 6.5 assists per game as a rookie. But the team lost Reeves for most of 1998–99 when he injured his back and remained stuck in a rut, going just 8–42 in a season that was shortened because of labor disputes between owners and players.

The Grizzlies kept searching for that special player who could turn their fortunes around, and in the 1999 NBA Draft, they nabbed guard Steve Francis, who was known for his quick slashing ability and highflying dunks. But Francis threw a wrench into Vancouver's plans by publicly announcing that he would not play for the lowly Grizzlies. So the Grizzlies orchestrated a 3-team, 11-player deal with the Houston Rockets and Orlando Magic that brought 4 players—forward Othella Harrington and guards Michael Dickerson, Brent Price, and Antoine Carr—and several future draft picks to Vancouver. Still, Vancouver's play on the court remained largely the same, and the 1999–2000 Grizzlies finished just 22–60.

On September 22, 2008, Shareef Abdur-Rahim retired from the NBA as one of the most underrated players of his time. Abdur-Rahim's career started when he left the University of California after only one year, and the Grizzlies selected the youngster with the third overall pick of the 1996 NBA Draft. He made an immediate impact in Vancouver as a silky-smooth scorer who could hit shots from anywhere on the court, setting a franchise record with an 18.7-points-per-game average as a rookie. In the 2000 Summer Olympics, he gained wider exposure by helping the United States' men's team capture the gold medal. In a 2000 interview, Abdur-Rahim talked about the pressure of taking shots in high-stakes games. "I think in those situations, I have enough guts to step up and take the shot, and if I make a mistake, I can deal with it. I don't look at basketball as pressure. Pressure is a man with a family and five kids and no job." Abdur-Rahim played in the NBA for 12 seasons (wearing the uniforms of 4 different teams) and was an All-Star in 2001–02.

SEEKING GREENER PASTURES

STROMILE SWIFT'S ENTERTAINING DUNKS BECAME KNOWN AS "THE STRO SHOW."

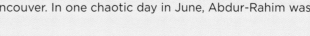hree new figures arrived in Vancouver in 2000. The first was head coach Sidney Lowe, who preached defense and teamwork as the keys to success. Also arriving in the Pacific Northwest were backup center Isaac Austin and rookie forward Stromile Swift. New general manager Billy Knight described the athletic, 6-foot-9 "Stro" as "a young colt ready to stand in the winner's circle."

Reeves' nagging injuries in 2000–01 limited his output, but his teammates did manage some modest accomplishments, including a then franchise-record five-game winning streak. Still, the negatives outweighed the positives as the team stumbled to a 23–59 finish. With every defeat, Vancouver fan support continued to dwindle.

After that sixth season, a major shake-up took place in Vancouver. In one chaotic day in June, Abdur-Rahim was

MIKE BIBBY

POSITION GUARD
HEIGHT 6-FOOT-1
GRIZZLIES SEASONS
1998–2001

In Mike Bibby's family, basketball ran in the blood. Bibby's father, Henry, had been an NBA point guard who later served as an assistant coach for the Philadelphia 76ers. Mike entered the pros in 1998, when the Grizzlies picked him second overall in the NBA Draft out of the University of Arizona. "With Bibby, you have a guy who is clearly the best player at that position in the draft, who knows how to run a team, and has excellent shooting ability," said Grizzlies president Stu Jackson. "Although he's young, he's probably going to be a real good point guard in the future." Bibby proved Jackson correct as he quickly established himself as an elite player with savvy playmaking abilities and a knack for hitting clutch shots. In his first year, the point guard made the NBA All-Rookie team and led the Grizzlies in both assists and steals. "He's consistent, he doesn't make mistakes, and he can run, too," said Los Angeles Lakers point guard Derek Fisher. In 2001, however, when retaining Bibby with a new contract became too expensive, the Grizzlies traded him to the Sacramento Kings.

traded to the Atlanta Hawks for the draft rights to Spanish forward/center Pau Gasol; the club drafted Duke University forward Shane Battier, the College Player of the Year; and Mike Bibby was sent to the Sacramento Kings in exchange for Jason Williams, one of the league's flashiest point guards. These additions revamped the Grizzlies' lineup, but the biggest change was still to come. Less than a week after the 2001 NBA Draft, the league approved the sale of the struggling Grizzlies to a group of businessmen in Memphis. So, the team said goodbye to the Pacific Northwest and moved from Canada to southwestern Tennessee.

The Memphis Grizzlies opened the 2001–02 season in their temporary home, the Pyramid Arena, with an eight-game losing streak. Halfway through the season, Reeves, still battling chronic back pain, retired after just six and a half NBA seasons. "Bryant has been a tremendous player and an exceptional team member, and we will certainly miss his contributions to our organization," Knight said. "We really appreciate his hard work and dedication to the team throughout the years."

Although the Grizzlies finished their inaugural Memphis season just 23–59, the play of Gasol—who averaged 17.6 points per game and won the NBA Rookie of the Year award by leading all first-year players in points, rebounds, and blocked shots—offered hope to the team's new fan base. Forward Lorenzen Wright, a former University of Memphis star, also impressed the hometown crowd with several big performances, including a 33-point effort against the Mavericks early in the season.

Before the 2002–03 season began, the Grizzlies brought in Jerry West, a longtime player, coach, and executive for the Los Angeles Lakers, as Memphis's new team president. "This opportunity gives me a challenge to do something unique," West said. "I have always wondered how it would be to build a winning franchise that has not experienced much success."

Success remained in short supply as the Grizzlies opened the next season with eight straight defeats, and Coach Lowe was fired. Under new coach Hubie Brown, a veteran of the NBA sidelines, the Grizzlies also lost the next five games. But in a home game against star guard Michael Jordan and the Washington Wizards, an unlikely hero emerged to end the drought. Second-year point guard Earl Watson came off the Memphis bench to score a career-high 17 points. In the fourth quarter, with the game tied and barely two minutes remaining, Watson nailed a three-pointer from the top of the key to give the Grizzlies the lead and spur them to an eventual 85–74 victory.

From there, the Grizzlies fought their way to a final mark of 28–54, their best yet. Gasol poured in 19 points a game to set the scoring pace, Williams led the team in assists, and forward Mike Miller, a former Rookie of the Year award winner with the Magic, added offensive spark with his long-range gunning. Although the team's eighth season ended with an eighth losing record, the Grizzlies seemed to finally be moving up.

BLUE EDWARDS

COURTSIDE STORIES

FEELING BLUE

Few teams play their way into the NBA record books in their very first season. The Vancouver Grizzlies did it—although not in the manner they might have hoped—with a 23-game losing streak that set the mark for the most consecutive losses in a single season. In 1996, between February 16 and April 2, the Grizzlies lost every single game. "Basically," Grizzlies guard Greg Anthony summed up during the streak, "we're a bad basketball team." It wasn't until they took on the Minnesota Timberwolves at home on April 3 that the Grizzlies decided enough was enough. Vancouver trailed by 12 points after 3 quarters. But the Grizzlies made a spectacular comeback by going on a 16–0 run, and then veteran forward Blue Edwards hit the game-winning shot from the top of the key with less than a second left on the clock. "I think we'd forgotten what it feels like to win," Edwards said amid the celebration that followed. The Grizzlies' dubious record was matched two years later by the 1997–98 Denver Nuggets.

WAKING FROM HIBERNATION

CLUTCH SCORER JAMES POSEY IGNITED MEMPHIS FANS' HOPES FOR A PLAYOFF RUN.

PAU GASOL

he Grizzlies' roar was heard in 2003–04, thanks in part to the addition of forwards James Posey and Bo Outlaw and the continued improvement of Watson. Memphis displayed a determination never before exhibited by the franchise, frequently turning second-half deficits into victories, and cruising to an unthinkable 50–32 mark and first-ever playoff appearance. The success was a true team effort, as 8 players averaged 20 minutes or more of playing time per game. "It's a great turnaround for the franchise," Gasol said about making the playoffs. "We've surprised ourselves. I can't believe where we are."

In the first round of the playoffs, the Grizzlies took on the defending NBA champion San Antonio Spurs, losing the first two games in San Antonio. In Game 3, the Grizzlies' first-ever home playoff game, Memphis trailed

MOVING TO MEMPHIS

In 1995, the Toronto Raptors and the Vancouver Grizzlies became the first big-time professional basketball teams to play in Canada since the Toronto Huskies in 1946. But basketball in Vancouver did not last long, and the Grizzlies never came close to a winning season in their six years there. Low morale among fans and decreasing support from the community left the team in debt, and by the year 2000, owner Michael Heisley had begun shopping for a new home for his team. In 2001, NBA owners unanimously approved the Grizzlies' relocation to Memphis, Tennessee. Memphis's acquisition of a pro sports franchise was a long time in coming; the city had been a finalist for a National Football League expansion team in 1974 and 1993 but lost out both times. "This is an exciting day for the people of Memphis," said J. R. Hyde, a part-owner of the team who had played a major role in bringing the club to Tennessee. "It's time to turn our focus to building a competitive basketball team that will be a positive force in the city."

95–93 with only seconds left in the fourth quarter. Miller launched a three-pointer that would have won the game, but the shot went just long of the rim as the buzzer sounded. That was as close as Memphis would get to a taste of playoff victory, as it dropped the next game to lose the series.

The Grizzlies were eager to achieve bigger and better things the next season, yet they struggled early. Then, unexpectedly, 71-year-old Hubie Brown resigned on Thanksgiving Day, stating that his health could no longer handle the daily strain of NBA coaching. The Grizzlies soon replaced him with Mike Fratello, former coach of the Hawks. Fratello's squad continued to struggle before a strong 12–3 midseason push propelled them to a 45–37 finish, good enough to claim the eighth spot in the Western Conference playoffs. Unfortunately, the Grizzlies were again swept in the first round, this time

JASON WILLIAMS (#2) BROUGHT A SCRAPPY, URBAN STYLE CALLED "STREETBALL" TO HIS GAME.

THE COMEBACK KIDS

The Memphis Grizzlies have struggled more years than not, often hoping to win merely 20 games in a season. But during the 2003–04 season, the Grizzlies became known throughout the NBA as the "Comeback Kids" as they rolled to an impressive 50–32 record. Memphis rallied to win 14 games when trailing after the third quarter, the most by any NBA team that season. In a January 19 game against the Houston Rockets, the Grizzlies trailed by eight in the fourth quarter, but forward James Posey rallied Memphis to a 16–2 run that won the game. "We just kept fighting and making big plays down the stretch," Posey said. "When it's crunch time, you have to be able to go for the ball, which we did tonight." Posey played the role of hero again on March 29 in a game against the Atlanta Hawks, scoring 38 points and hitting a buzzer-beating 3-pointer to force a second overtime en route to a 136–133 Grizzlies victory. "We refused to lose," said Posey. Eighteen days later, the Comeback Kids made their first-ever playoff appearance.

"WE ACQUIRED ONE OF THE VERY BEST PROSPECTS FROM THIS YEAR'S DRAFT. EVEN THOUGH HE IS A VERY YOUNG PLAYER AT 19, THE TALENT OF THIS YOUNG MAN IS PHENOMENAL."

— JERRY WEST ON RUDY GAY

by the Phoenix Suns. "It's hard right now," Gasol said after Memphis fell 123–115 in Game 4. "Maybe after watching and seeing yourself [in a replay of the game] you can learn, but right now it is just painful."

he Grizzlies continued to stockpile talent in the off-season, selecting Hakim Warrick, a swift, 6-foot-9 forward from Syracuse University, in the 2005 NBA Draft. Two months later, on August 2, the Grizzlies took part in the biggest trade in NBA history, a swap involving 13 players from 5 teams. In this mega-blockbuster deal, Memphis sent Posey and Williams to the Miami Heat for veteran guard Eddie Jones. In another deal, forward Bonzi Wells was shipped to the Kings for scrappy point guard Bobby Jackson.

The moves seemed to pay off early in the 2005–06 season, as the Grizzlies claimed victory in 13 of their first 18 games. But playing in the same division (now the Southwest) as the perennial powerhouse Spurs and Mavericks, the Grizzlies wound up in third place with 49 wins. The mark put the Grizzlies back in the playoffs,

but, once again, the Memphis faithful watched their club get swept in a four-game series, this time by the Mavericks.

The Grizzlies continued to tinker with their roster, trading Battier to the Houston Rockets for Stromile Swift (who returned to the team for a second stint) and 6-foot-9 rookie forward Rudy Gay. "We acquired one of the very best prospects from this year's draft," Jerry West said of Gay. "Even though he is a very young player at 19, the talent of this young man is phenomenal, and we are hopeful people will enjoy watching this kind of athlete."

PAU GASOL

POSITION FORWARD / CENTER
HEIGHT 7 FEET
GRIZZLIES SEASONS
2001–08

Pau Gasol was a force to be reckoned with. Standing 7 feet tall and weighing 227 pounds, this Spanish native could move, pour in baskets from the post, rebound, and even knock down free throws with great accuracy. He was often compared to another multitalented NBA star, forward Kevin Garnett, for his ability to handle the ball and create plays off the dribble. "I think he's very versatile, a high basketball IQ, can pass, can shoot, catch, finish ... he's extremely talented," said star Los Angeles Lakers guard Kobe Bryant. In 2001, Gasol arrived in Memphis as the third overall pick in the NBA Draft, becoming (at the time) the highest-drafted foreign player ever. "It's the best day of my life," Gasol said. "All of my life I want to be in the NBA." Gasol didn't waste any time making his mark as he won Rookie of the Year honors while ranking ninth in the NBA in blocked shots per game. He remained a lethal low-post scorer for the Grizzlies for the next five seasons until he was traded to the Lakers in 2008.

RAISING A
NEW LITTER

MIKE MILLER'S VERSATILITY EARNED HIM THE 2005–06 SIXTH MAN OF THE YEAR AWARD.

HAKIM WARRICK

The 2006–07 Grizzlies' playoff hopes were effectively squelched before the season even began, as Gasol broke his left foot while playing for Spain in the summertime International Basketball Federation World Championship. He would miss the first 22 games of the season, and the Grizzlies went 5–17 in his absence. At the end of December, Coach Fratello was fired. Tony Barone, the team's personnel director, filled in, but with such instability, the Grizzlies ended up with an NBA-worst 22–60 record. Still, there were some bright spots. Gay gave glimpses of his potential by averaging 10.8 points per game, and Gasol—once he returned from his injury—set career highs with 20.8 points and 9.8 boards a night.

In the off-season, the Grizzlies hired former Suns assistant coach Marc Iavaroni as their 10th head coach. The team also acquired 6-foot-3 guard Juan Carlos Navarro, a

THE NEW DEN

On November 3, 2004, the Grizzlies started a new season in a new home: the FedExForum, a $250-million, state-of-the-art arena built for the team on famous Beale Street in the heart of Memphis's entertainment district. The arena was built with fine dining options, a sports bar, and the latest stadium technology. Because Memphis is renowned for its contributions to the blues and rock 'n' roll, the theme of Memphis music decorates the interior. There are hallways dedicated to gospel, blues, rock, rap, hip-hop, and original artwork from regional artists representing the music of Memphis. "A forum is a public place, and this arena will be a showcase for professional sports and family entertainment that will serve the Memphis area for years to come," said FedEx executive vice president Michael Glenn. On that opening night of November 3, a capacity crowd of 18,119 hoped to see the Grizzlies crush the Washington Wizards, but the home team lost, 103–91. Memphis fans had to wait until November 10 to see a home victory, when forward Stromile Swift and his teammates topped the Los Angeles Lakers, 110–87.

"GUYS ARE REALLY BUYING INTO WHAT COACH HAS BEEN TELLING US, AND AFTER YOU SEE TEAM BASKETBALL GETS YOU WINS, GUYS MAKE IT A POINT TO WORK ON IT."

— MIKE CONLEY ON 2008–09 PROGRESS

27-year-old rookie from Spain who was known as a capable marksman and tough defender.

Unfortunately, the new Grizzlies looked a lot like the old ones, as the team sputtered to a 5–10 start in 2007–08. Still mired in a losing funk by the beginning of February, Memphis traded its best player, Gasol, to the Lakers for 7-foot-1 center Marc Gasol (Pau's younger brother), 6-foot-11 center Kwame Brown, and guards Javaris Crittenton and Aaron McKie, plus first-round draft picks in 2008 and 2010. "We're a 13-win team, so when you're in that situation, you've got to make moves," explained Chris Wallace, who had replaced West as general manager in 2007. The Grizzlies would win just nine more games that season.

Memphis kept wheeling and dealing as it sought a winning combination. In the 2008 NBA Draft, the club swung a trade, sending Miller and rookie forward Kevin Love to the Minnesota Timberwolves for 6-foot-4 guard O. J. Mayo. Mayo was an offensive dynamo who had netted 20.7 points per game during his single year at the University of Southern California. After also obtaining burly rookie forward Darrell Arthur, the Grizzlies went into the 2008–09 season with one of the NBA's

youngest lineups—the average Memphis starter was a mere 21 years old.

As had become typical, the Grizzlies struggled early in the season. A month into the schedule, however, they started to turn things around. On December 14, Memphis defeated the Miami Heat behind Mayo's 28 points, notching its fourth victory in a row. "Guys are really buying into what Coach [Marc Iavaroni] has been telling us," said Grizzlies point guard Mike Conley. "And after you see team basketball gets you wins, guys make it a point to work on it."

As the season played out, the explosive Mayo led all NBA first-year players with 18.5 points per game. Gasol proved himself a mean inside force, Gay emerged as Memphis's "go-to" scorer in clutch situations, and Warrick developed into an outstanding sixth man, adding hustle and soaring dunks as he came into games off the bench. Still, the Grizzlies' inexperience showed as they finished 24–58. Toward season's end, assistant coach Lionel Hollins took over head coaching duties.

HUBIE BROWN

COACH
GRIZZLIES SEASONS
2002–04

For more than half a century, Hubert "Hubie" Brown committed himself fully to basketball, starting with an amateur playing career while in the U.S. Army in the 1950s. He then moved into the coaching ranks, eventually leading the Atlanta Hawks from 1976 to 1981 and the New York Knicks from 1982 to 1987. He retired from coaching in 1988 and worked as a television broadcaster until 2002, when the Grizzlies persuaded him to once again pick up the coaching whistle. As the NBA's oldest coach at 69 years of age, he turned the Grizzlies around with his patient, instructional coaching style. During the 2003–04 season, the Grizzlies went 50–32 and made the playoffs for the first time in franchise history. "What Hubie Brown has done for our league in the last two years has been great," said Indiana Pacers coach Rick Carlisle. "He brought an injection of life into that Memphis franchise and made them a playoff team." Late in 2004, however, health problems forced Brown to hang up his coaching whistle again. The following year, he was inducted into the Basketball Hall of Fame.

Hollins was given more tools to work with before the 2009–10 season, when Memphis drafted shot-blocking center Hasheem Thabeet, and traded for big-bodied forward Zach Randolph. Randolph earned his paycheck, becoming the club's leading scorer and rebounder. The Grizzlies started their 15th season with a 1–8 whimper, but they were soon piling up victories, improving to 25–21 by the end of January. "Zach has been the catalyst behind our turnaround," Wallace said. "Other teams have to double-team him, so there's more room out there for O. J. Mayo and Rudy Gay to operate." The Grizzlies then cooled down and missed an invitation to the playoffs. Even so, the young talent in Memphis had fans hopeful for what lay ahead.

NICKNAMED "HELICOPTER," HIGHFLYING HAKIM WARRICK USED A 38-INCH LEAP TO REACH THE RIM.

FOR THE THIRD SEASON IN A ROW, O. J. MAYO LED THE 2010–11 GRIZZLIES IN THREE-POINTERS, WITH 96.

POSTSEASON BREAKTHROUGH

MARC GASOL'S LANKY BUILD HELPED HIM BECOME DEFENSIVE PLAYER OF THE YEAR BY 2012-13.

Memphis saw little need to break up the core of Randolph, Gay, Mayo, Gasol, and Conley heading into the 2010–11 campaign. But the club did add depth and championship experience by signing guard Tony Allen, a defensive specialist who'd earned a 2008 title ring with the Boston Celtics. Randolph had a remarkable year, tallying 20.1 points and 12.2 boards per contest, and Conley posted career highs in points, assists, and steals.

By mid-February of 2011, the Grizzlies were cruising when Gay suffered a season-ending shoulder injury. The loss of the dependable star could have ruined the bruins, but Memphis fought on to a 46–36 finish. The record was good enough to earn Memphis the lowest playoff spot in the Western Conference. Slated to play the 61–21 Spurs, the Grizzlies' chances of overturning their terrible

41

postseason history seemed slim. But the upstart Grizzlies shocked the battle-tested Spurs when they came away with a Game 1 victory in San Antonio. The postseason win was the first in franchise history, and the Grizzlies weren't finished yet. They took two of the next four games as well. Then in Game 6, Randolph sealed the series upset with a 31-point, 11-rebound performance. "Emotion is high, not just for the Memphis Grizzlies but for the whole city of Memphis and the fans," Randolph said. "It's a great accomplishment....

[but] we've got a game Sunday, and we have to get ready."

The confident Grizzlies were ready for the next game and defeated the equally young Oklahoma City Thunder on the road. After five more meetings, including overtime and triple overtime bouts, the clubs were even, at three games apiece. But in Game 7, Thunder forward Kevin Durant torched the Grizzlies for 39 points and ended their unlikely playoff run.

In 2011–12, Gay was back, and Memphis looked better than ever, plowing through a

RUDY GAY

POSITION FORWARD
HEIGHT 6-FOOT-9
GRIZZLIES SEASONS
2006–13

"Rudy! Rudy! Rudy!" The Memphis forward with the name fans loved to chant also had talent worthy of such vocal outcries. Rudy Gay combined size and explosive athleticism with smooth body control. He could score inside, outside, and on the break, and he was also a solid defender and rebounder. In just his second pro season, Gay averaged 20.1 points, 6.2 rebounds, 1.4 steals, and a block per game. To complement his physical talents, Gay quickly developed the mental maturity needed at the pro level. At just 22, Gay already had more NBA experience than many of his teammates and was depended upon to set the tone for the inexperienced club. "Rudy's proven that he's willing to adapt more than anything," teammate Mike Conley said. "He's learned how to deal with double teams and how to play off of other people. He's doing things other than scoring. But he's still the kind of guy who loves to take and make big shots. He loves the pressure." When he left the club in 2013, Gay had suited up for the Grizzlies more times than any other player.

INSIDE MAN ZACH RANDOLPH WAS NAMED AN ALL-STAR FOR THE SECOND TIME IN 2013.

KILLER CUBS

In the NBA, it is difficult to select, develop, and keep young talent. But beginning in 2006, the Memphis Grizzlies made it look easy. Memphis acquired rookie small forward Rudy Gay that year and drafted point guard Mike Conley the next. Three more rookies—shooting guard O. J. Mayo (pictured), center Marc Gasol, and power forward Darrell Arthur—joined in 2008. Aside from a couple veterans added later, this quintet became the Grizzlies' core for several years, and the club's win percentage rose each season from 2007–08 to 2011–12. The relatively unknown up-and-comers took the spotlight in the 2011 playoffs. Gay was sidelined with an injury, but the others demonstrated a cohesiveness that belied their age, pulling off a huge series upset over the top-ranked San Antonio Spurs, a team full of veteran stars. "We were hoping at some point that they would fold under the pressure, make some mistakes … and they didn't," Spurs forward Tim Duncan said. "They did the exact opposite…. they took care of the ball, they got the shots they wanted to get, and their guys made the shots when they needed to."

> "EMOTION IS HIGH, NOT JUST FOR THE MEMPHIS GRIZZLIES BUT FOR THE WHOLE CITY OF MEMPHIS AND THE FANS. IT'S A GREAT ACCOMPLISHMENT.... [BUT] WE'VE GOT A GAME SUNDAY, AND WE HAVE TO GET READY."
>
> — ZACH RANDOLPH ON A 2011 PLAYOFF WIN

lockout-shortened season to a 41–25 record. Going into the 2012 playoffs, the Grizzlies were no longer underdogs, and their full arsenal of players was available. Unfortunately, the Los Angeles Clippers, led by forward Blake Griffin and guard Chris Paul, spoiled the Grizzlies' postseason. Memphis lost two contests by a single point and another game in overtime on their way to a first-round dismissal from the playoffs. Mayo left town after the season.

The Grizzlies channeled their disappointment into renewed focus in 2012–13, streaking to a 12–2 start. In midseason, Memphis reluctantly dealt the expensive Gay away. But in return, the Grizzlies received three tall, active forwards, including Ed Davis and Tayshaun Prince. The trade added depth and helped the Grizzlies form the stingiest defense in the league. After a franchise-best 56 wins, Memphis faced the Clippers once again in the playoffs. After losses in the first two games of the series, Randolph led the Grizzlies to four straight victories. Memphis then bested the top-seeded Thunder in five games to advance to the Western Conference finals, where it was unseated by the Spurs.

Western Conference wins were tough to come by the following season despite the fearless play of Randolph and Conley on both ends of the floor. Prince and sharpshooting guard Courtney Lee rounded out the lineup, even as a knee injury benched Gasol for the early part of the season. Rather than dwell on the loss, some players saw the hole in the offense as an opportunity to step up their game. New coach Dave Joerger was especially impressed with Randolph, saying, "He's a guy who's always double-teamed but creates shots for other people."

After the club's inception in Vancouver two decades ago, the Grizzlies seemingly spent their first several seasons in hibernation. Even bear-sized Bryant Reeves couldn't give the club much bite. Hard times followed the Grizzlies to cotton country, but today's Grizzlies have at last bared their fangs and are determined to become the next great headliners to come out of Memphis.

INDEX